THE DIRTY KNEES OF PRAYER

Caitlin Press Inc.
8100 Alderwood Road, Halfmoon Bay, BC V0N 1Y1
www.caitlin-press.com

Text design by Amy Thuy Do and Vici Johnstone
Cover design and photo by Vici Johnstone
Printed in Canada
Caitlin Press Inc. acknowledges financial support from the
Government of Canada and the Canada Council for the Arts, and from
the Province of British Columbia through the British Columbia Arts
Council and the Book Publisher's Tax Credit.

Library and Archives Canada Cataloguing in Publication

Shay, Timothy, 1952-, author

    The dirty knees of prayer / Timothy Shay.

 Poems.

ISBN 978-1-987915-08-2 (paperback)

    I. Title.

PS8587.H37D57 2016   C811'.54   C2015-908099-1

THE DIRTY KNEES OF PRAYER

TIMOTHY SHAY

CAITLIN PRESS

For Megan

BONSAI: Epigraph

uncertain is the word but i won't use it again
this clay vessel contains it
and darkness describes it
there must be something behind those eyes
in the dark
and the breakdown   sees us shattered
several chunks like cupped hands
catch the water   the beach rain
a lake licking at our roots
tendrils exposed   pink and thinking

~Timmy wept this morning because the flowers are dead. A
heavy frost came last night and froze them. He mourns them as
he would a very dear friend; he loved them so. He said, "I said
good-bye to them yesterday and now they are dead."~

— *Betty Shay, Journal entry. September 21st 1957*
Keno, Yukon.

CONTENTS

THE DIRTY KNEES OF PRAYER — ONE

with thanks to W. Enewold
for Jeffrey Dean Shay

It's morning on Muffin Street. There goes the fat man, shaped
like an egg, trundling down. He wears a bright red hat and
carries a large yellow bag. This is my breakfast I think, my
breakfast haunting me. He looks up at my high window with his
little peppercorn eyes. Treats my deep seclusion like some kind
of yolk …

Apparently when I start again, fresh and pink, all shit and squall,
I will be encumbered with vague memories of the unfinished
mess I produced this time around. Everything without a file.
Scrambled papers on the floor, a porridge of forgotten crops
settled into the bottom tray of my old white Inglis refrigerator.

According to one quantum physicist this idea of directional
movement is a delusion. No intent behind the motion of time,
no inextricable plodding forward as if to some goal. Apparently
the billion times I repeat the phenomena of shitting and
squalling helplessness, all billion are simultaneous. Even with
the distracting security of the ready breast.

This physicist (hiding in his house) claims quantum theory
gave us concepts essential to the cd player the dvd and the
computerized world wide web and because they function,
quantum theory pursued indicates there must be billions of
versions of each of us, housed in billions of very real worlds.
Each of the billions of each of us are simultaneously deciding
what to do next.

One of me sees a man acting like breakfast; another eats eggs that look like the eyeballs of a surprised person; another me chokes on dry toast and falls down stairs breaking his neck; the next just suffocates on the same wad of toast and some other one of us falls asleep, face first in the plate, blowing happy antediluvian bubbles in the Heinz ketchup.

The physicist says that if this is not the case then something more bizarre must be. I get the creeps and choose a day in my goose down quilt calling out like a loon on a Yukon lake. I figure one of us must do something like this while the others take their turns dying. Quantum mechanics seems to allow dementia in lieu of paid holidays. Let's start over:

CROW IN HIS DARK UNIFORM

Crow asleep is a hill
dark slope of wings
pasture called night

Deep black
as holes in cosmos
eyes two lost planets
in separate orbit

Crow in speech
is the squall
of some tiny dark hurricane
called birth

Crow in his dark uniform
marches the sky named day
taxes the rooted inhabitants
with shrill orders
and intricate procedures of drill

THE DIRTY KNEES OF PRAYER — TWO

Sitting on the edge of my bed. Looking out the window.
Thoughts that make me want to puke course through my head.
Thoughts like "a river winds through everything."

Thinking this reminds me of the health food store lineup. They
have the only brand of chai tea I like so I find myself in a lineup
of the well-meaning. Slow as corn syrup ... sticky sweet. The
proprietor and some timeless hippy woman chatter in perky
tones, speak of the shifting planets, the influence of the moon,
the song of birds, an impending astrological shift at 3am into the
darkness. "O heavens no! Not the darkness," says the proprietor.
The beady hippy doesn't miss a beat, says "O yes, the positive
darkness, the quiet darkness." Proprietor, "Yes, positive, good,
healing darkness ... " Sounds like politicians making an effort to
rationalize something distasteful. Sounds like death to me.

Looking out my window and an old truck shoots from the
ally onto the main street. It has a yellow hood and a red body.
Well past breakfast time. I saw the fat man today, dressed as
an autumnally prepared lumberjack. He had developed a long
stride to go with his red plaid shirt. Even the lamp posts looked
vaguely like trees.

WAILING WALL

How grand
of the old fart
to spend the morning with me
over coffee
discussing literature
with little Corina standing there
as he says
o Corina
i who am alone and to this moment
singular

Snow did not give
yellow leaves the time to depart
the mountain side appears stained
with golden piss patches

After a time
this landscape sways you
moulds you until the world's mountains
appear as minor hills on
a toy globe spinning
with the people's constant preoccupations
their wailing wall   their cloud catcher

THE DIRTY KNEES OF PRAYER — THREE: CRUMBS

Somewhere in the ether floats an idea. Tiny as a dust mite and just as ugly. Folded in on its beauty like a confused origami. The sweet vaulting song emerges from the throats of the slaves of G-d and somehow they seem convincingly happy as if their self-imposed limitations, their cloistered inhibitions, were the source of freedom from some nagging worry, the clawing hungry, the raped and the raped again. And how this lack of belief and dedication is the alum that makes my morning smile. Expectant, humanistic, yet masking an army of teeth. Ready to gnash.

Somewhere along the line I got lost and realized I had never had a thing to say. Now I mumble to myself a lot and demand the Earless Infinite return my stolen house, call on my dead great-aunt to adjust the lottery results and help me buy my stolen house back and its fruit trees, its gardens. It is as close as I come to the dirty knees of prayer.

There is this theoretical bottom we can hit yet I continue in free fall through the wet atmosphere. There is so much time to think and though I was never issued a parachute I remember encouraging stories of World War II pilots abandoning flaming planes and falling four miles onto a little bush, which apparently was just enough to save every bone in the pilot's body. But as the wind whips by and the rain lashes my face, I know secretly that I have fallen further than four tiny miles. When I woke up on Saturday I was suspended in a mulberry tree. The monkey said, "Yer sure a lucky cat!" I never leave my house because I am alone. The world is not safe. The adventure I wanted is not in a book. The fish I dream of detests the hook. My father roasted the tongues of cattle in our oven and said this is like corned beef. He told me what was really in wieners and stole the picnic I still search for. I left my house and they stole it too. I want it back.

I rode a bicycle along the river. I sang a song. I said, "Why can't we make it better?" With Band-Aids. Yesterday I saw Band-Aids in a store window. The design printed on them made them look like strips of bacon. I thought I would send some bacon-Band-Aids at Christmas to all Jews and Islamic peoples with a message encouraging Christian healing. Why do good intentions so often fail?

I had a dream not too long ago and I was very happy. My heart condition had disappeared, some fool had bought my broken van and I had lots of money, which I'd found in an abandoned paper bag. Life was looking pretty good. Even my ex-wife had found someone else to focus on. My crazy prodigal daughter had become dictator of Wyoming and wanted to buy me a fast car. I could see again and felt no obligation to praise the Lord. I could chew once my teeth had been ransomed from some evil fairy. Everything was looking up and I wasn't even worried about being loved … as I say, I had a dream …

And now I ride my bicycle attached to a generator, which makes my TV work. It is my way of saving the world. I think of the past constantly and bake things that only my dead grandmother knew how to make. I keep thinking in a disjointed kind of way that it's time for something new.

PRAYER

Bits of paper   ash
open eyeglass case

The overhead lamp
cbc radio are
some kind of old cronies
officials with calendars
fail to rename the hours yet

So it is dark on the
bus of strangers
Shuttled to work
before dawn
then home
again as night falls

Rain descends
sleep presses
appetite flees
prayer always pointless

THE DIRTY KNEES OF PRAYER — FOUR: CRUMBY

Today, no idea is a good one. The clouds clamour like nervous tarot cards. Everything seems to mean several things. Everything does mean several things. Simple devices refuse to cooperate. My toothbrush leaps from the shelf to toilet baptism. It is obviously not appropriate to think of the similarity between my body and an October squash abandoned in some damp field. Like me. Now, I catch sight of myself entering my funnel-shaped pants and though never a good idea I think of my father in ancient times watching TV on the couch. His vast belly shiny with whatever greasy thing he'd been eating. As a teenager it was the most disgusting sight imaginable. I thought if I ever looked like that I'd kill myself. So I've had to reconsider. Even though there are no advantages anymore, and they've stolen my house, and my daughter, The Dictator of Wyoming, directs the fate of nations from her dumpster office. I have decided to seize the day, have no ideas, and don't even think of relief, joy, ecstasy, love-making, inclusion, world peace or the inflated price of my favoured fatty pork chops.

The tennis shoes on the side of the road, mysteriously deposited, mysteriously unclaimed. The stupid drunk poet needed a ride so leapt in front of the speeding car. They say his body shot out of his shoes so quick that the shoes stood there for hours, exactly where he'd stood, as if waiting. Waiting. Apparently there is no need for shoes in the House of Jim Morrison. The stupid drunk poet sits there now, on a cloudy bench. He has applied for some eternal job tending the diaphanous tables of the dead.

My hangover memory, my hangnail, my brother hanging, hanging fruit, hung juries, well-hung daydreams. A shrug. A grunt. A snooze.

Once dreams were hopeful things, augurs, signs, omens. Now, awake and asleep I have little idea of meaning or direction. I am the type who wanders aimlessly. My day is a success if I find a penny in the traffic lane. Horns honk like trumpets. Drivers yell like peasants ... my blind, alcoholic and dead grandfather drives by, whipping the ghostly horse that pulls his demented carriage down the freeway. He is always off to the races.

Hangover and hangnail conspire against me. My brother the Houdini of Suicide managed to hang his entire six foot four inch body from a beam in a six foot tall shed. The night before he died he told a Mormon Elder that he'd really like to meet Jesus as he had a few things to ask him. The hanging fruit falls wasp-ridden and rotten to the ground near my stolen house while the world starves. The world an indecisive hung jury where passion is replaced by daydream, bug eyed and lascivious down the long staircase of chronological decomposition. I am guilty. I am sentenced. I thank G-d for my daily pills ... Sometimes I feel almost normal.

White rented party tents. Knights in garters, Ladies in their cups. Those who continue to marry and those who continue to look to the G-d of blood revenge for simple solace ... I burned the rice pilaf. The pork chop is tough. This shrimp scampi tastes like fish! One daughter suffers burdens of real sorrow. Another daughter has tattooed lips and studies the arrangement of flowers. The third ascended to the secret crown of Wyoming. (As her court clerk I prepared a genealogy. When I demonstrated that our family tree went all the way back to mythology and here, see, your 68th great grandmother was a Valkyrie ... she said ... "Finally! About time you found someone interesting.") Her train of rags raises the applause of dust and a tintinnabulation of pebbles. She knows the forgotten martyrs of Heroin and the Pope of Pop Cans. I appeal to her for a title. She gives me a fiefdom and calls me Keeper of the Ashes of Sentimentality, Purveyor of Honey Nut Cheerios and the Queen Daddy. I am satisfied. Everything is so tragic I have learned to laugh along with the great tragic comedians, the not-so-funny clowns, the slapstick of dirty dish solitude. I mutter a lot about getting the joke ... how the punchline winded me when it hit me in the gut. Most days I see stars. Real nice.

A very specific destination in no particular direction. Plot is a plot. Plot is the sound of a slow heavy rain stealing your time with its sleepy song. Plot, plot, plot, the sound of your wet shoes strolling home from walking on water. Again and again you've walked on water but only when the faithless are asleep. Plot is conspiracy.

Beginning, middle, end, climax, anti-climax, resolution. How is the masterpiece chained to a presupposed outcome? If there's no story there's nothing to lie about. And can't you see I'm telling the truth now that my brother has finally taught himself to be quiet for long enough to listen to my sonorous wisdom ... my inflated rubber pontification?

THE SUMMER SHE WAS NOT

Filled up with deer trail
foliage of emily carr
cliffs taller than cities

Down travelling
he came to the edge
of mountain lake
filled with emptiness
of bus
the lack
of animal movement
in roadside forest
hung

The summer she was not
filled with heat
or awaited bathing suit
but dim sweeping rains
brushstroked the edge
of granite deep cultus lake
inland   somehow prone
he walked

Unravelled the mystery
of drift wood
dead fish
trees wavering and washed
painted
in a summer of hidden flies
mosquitoes plentiful
as raindrops

The summer she was not
is a mere ghost
a grey cloud or vision
of smoke

Wavers
on the lake edge of memory
absence

MAGIC BEANS

No one but a fool consents to trade his talent for a joke.
— Marie de France circa 1300 AD

1.

He rambles in the hope of gathering spilled soup.
He has asked for the viscous essence of legume
to gather itself together in a compliant yoga of bowls
but the remains remain really relaxed, spread out flat,
like an afternoon dream during a nap, collapsed,
no steam no attractive porcelain enclosure
shining spoon, tablecloth, well set room,
place of ritual, where we all begin and forever end.

2.

Often during this lifetime
my body has felt something like a gourd
or squash, a glorious seasonal pumpkin,
as prone to erosion as Cinderella's midnight coach

And now the vast jungle of the garden is yellowed
begins to dissolve in the chill and damp
so I check for soft frost spots on my leathery skin
this body I'm cradled in   I feel for cracks
where my thinking and focussed obsession
has stumbled   fallen hard against the stubborn earth,
head cracked on the stone pillow of ascending dreams,
the nightmare hard ax of my many executions by love.

Some days I am squashed
my gait cucumberous
I recall my slim and seemingly immortal zucchini legs
I recall with brains now ill-defined as steamed
spaghetti squash and yes I am ready,
so very tired and imagining
vague possibilities of a sudden thrill,
rescue from the collapse of the browning field,
some presentation at a sumptuous feast,
surprise to surprise the dull jade and shadow
of a formerly infamous and dangerous man.

3.

There is a mist over Vancouver
foghorns call in the voice of toads
from across the harbour
the horns of foreign ships
celebrate their obscurity
streets are slug slippery
parks mossy swamps
boggy deserted emporia
of past summer's picnic
... mist over Vancouver
a man clatters by on his blinking bicycle.
In the corners where dark night
stores its darker hollows
park benches are filled
with silence and the homeless in paradise.

In and out of obscurity and shadow
we see the form of what we think we're following
but it is just another crumb
on the trail to the deepest of green-woods.
"Hansel hansel" whisper breezes,
rattle of "Gretel" reply the leaves
and there the sweet iron oven of passage
god's little cookies
shrivelled sugar plums
suspended paper party lamps along
the steep path of ragged ascension

… a transit stop this life …
One more bus departing
another house, another wife,
sequential attempts at survivable life.
Necks craned in the mist and kerbside rain.
Eyes all squint as we lean
to the hissing arrival of our lighted number
our empty midnight train.

4.

You all seem as ugly as me
and just as distraught.
Your long faces on the bus
falling on and falling off
you're all heading somewhere now
up the street or down the hall and
when your destination completes
you'll leave no trace on empty streets

just a history of holey socks
torn webs of bed sheet
waving banners across the kingdom of night
where sans sunglasses you've sought the light

You all seem lost as me
kowtowing to buy cheque-to-cheque immortality
using your moment to get somewhere
and finally arriving
minus teeth and missing hair
but there ... most definitely there.

5.

He is occupied with finding his sand castle
washed away one day in the cobalt Pacific tide
scrubbing the dirt off his sedimentary memories
polishing them down to the smoothest curve
of petrified wood
making sure they're somehow good
worthy of the celebration ... and anecdotal recollection

He is occupied with his crop
of fresh disappointment.
It was a good year ... his orchard of blues songs
heavy with sacs of tart cool juice
rows of Shakespearean tragedies
so dark and so deeply Payne's grey
requiring a crew of slow and sorrowful migrant workers
to harvest them, to bend and collect the magic beans ...
yes magic beans ... always the hope of magic beans.

MONSTER

When i named the monsters
in my fragile length of life
and when i observed a multitude of stars
that had been seen before

I felt i was a conqueror
yet my smallness was that
of drifting dandelion seed

And the polytheism of the trees
the aromatic pulse of living compost
belittle that part of me
the conqueror
and namer of tiny monsters

BLACK ICE

tonight i am frightened by shadows
by ghost and thin layer of ice
disguised as road

it is two a.m.
i am driving my snow white toyota
there are threatening phone calls waiting at my house
and i am completely sober

THE SPIDERY ARMS OF SHRI TARA DEVI

She arrived an agent of Maha Kali Ma
in her blue lotus projection of Tara.
Spider woman Yaga shadows crowd
the close corridors like a vapour
of missing birds
where his bodhisattva walks.
She came with the prescribed tests
and trick questions;
A ventriloquy of hunting whistles
whisper her lessons,
this alphabet of footprints
where his bodhisattva walks.
She came to the fatty feast
of primordial meat.
Roasts, drippings and sauces of blood
papers and tablecloths stained with spilled gravy
shooting stars
where his bodhisattva eats.
He answered all the trick questions
and hurled himself at the tide of tests
and now in success he is alone,
his spine a curved path
where his bodhisattva passes
She went as an agent of Maha Kali Ma
sweeping the dirty path as it disappeared behind her
so he could never follow
into that jungle where his bodhisattva's heart
is the gate before the primal forest.
She came as a detective of Yaga agency
dealt the two-faced cards of royal houses naturally
juggled black holes and stars,
which light my bodhisattva's scissors
of detachment.

She came disguised in smiles and left in smiles.
Being so surprised
somehow makes him seem half restored
as he squints to observe his bodhisattva
in her favoured form dancing
amid the glints of dust
hovering in sunlight
as we grind the bones
to a dark paste
and speak of the perfect application
of foreign spices and
we laugh like an old joke.
Again, his bodhisattva teaches him
it is all a punchline arriving.

So he is almost an old man
when her eyes flag him down,
arrest him beside her highway of ambush
where yellow straw
and gophers animate the receding horizon.

CALYPSO MYTH

calypso has a body of pomegranate
sweet as all the sunsets we remember
she dances in the hilled woods beyond our town

it is her island

her nights are dark caves
and the few men who find her
are never seen again

yet there are those
who continue to search ...

BAIT

Today I discovered the horrible dark secret
of escalators and other things.
Anomalies like popcorn strung on a string
along the electric transit route;
a puzzling day made of many bits of poems,
crumbs of light, discarded castaways
of a retired feast   flickering Chinese lanterns

Just last year, I bragged to my friend,
of how I had ridden the escalator to the end
without lifting my feet
(I usually do a little leap)
necessitated by a fiction preserved from childhood
and my ill-founded fear
of being sucked into the escalator
or at the very least terribly maimed
by the tight metal lips and teeth
at the escalator's long mouth.

I planted my feet, closed my eyes and
surfed across   without incident.

Then this morning I discovered station workers
had removed all the steps
from the same escalator
that had hosted my daring stunt
and the absence of stairs exposed
a deep black hole
a shaft beneath the escalator
and at the end of it,
far below the escalator's mouth
a large pile of pee-yellow newspaper,
discarded transit tickets,

a sad semi-digested heap,
of several suits of
children's colourful clothes.

It was too early for my train so
I sat outside the Chinese fast food stand,
which hadn't opened yet,
but exuded the fragrance of freshly fried food and spice
through the slightly open door

When from across the station
a large man of sixty-five or so
sloughed toward me and announced,
"Sir, sometimes they are nice to me, Sir,
there in the Chinese food stand and
they give me extra lemon chicken,
but when this happens, Sir,
I can't help but weeping for joy, Sir,
so they stopped giving me extra chicken, Sir."

As he spoke he began to weep
huge splashing blue tears
a Yukon rain storm with drops
as big as buckets.
His sobbing astonished me.

He spoke through his precipitations,
"Sir, as you can see I'm very sensitive
and so I've never been able to marry.
But I went to a website
called 'plenty of fish'
and one hundred Caucasian women

and fifty Asian women
answered my ad even though I'm old, Sir,
older than you, and very sensitive, Sir,
so when I arranged to meet
my 'catch of the day',
I wept within seconds of sitting down
at the cafe table;
My date abruptly excused herself
and disappeared ... I keep weeping, Sir."

Then my train arrived
so I circumnavigated the predatory escalator,
and left the man who wept, waiting for chicken,
and later

I saw a large golden dragon on top of
a Buddhist temple near Pender Street
and there were two fat black crows resting
on the dragon's tail ... watching the approach
of new rain from the west.

I wondered what it all meant
and why it was contained
in just one day?

Then to the army and navy store,
where I bought a small casting crab trap
and permitted myself to dream
of standing on the long wooden pier in White Rock:
large raindrops falling,
a wind with a voice,
a month with an "R" in it,

whisky in the bitter thermos coffee,
casting one small net
into the vast undulation of Semiahmoo Bay.
My trap
a wallflower at some slow dance
of orange Dungeness
through a theatre of saline element,
green ticker tape …

Scuttling sideways with the clear focus
of appetite.
Drawn to the attractive presentation
at the core of the net,
that raw heart of delectable bait.

CANTO:
FROM A MAN WHO LOST HIS MOUTH TO SURGERY

The missing movement of my lips,
oceanic, engaged in deepest kiss,
a flotsam of gently twined tongues.

Luigi, harry, mike and barry
eaten by water body, removed
by cold lake, as bait
is removed by swift fish, as food
is removed by mouth, as mouth
was removed surgically,
snip snip snip, snip snip snip.

Missing grinding of rush hour teeth,
this ghost of smiling jaw still there,
a mastication of air by air.

THE WINE DARK SEA

1.

He held a gallon jar above his head
Graceful as an Olympic diver at five he dove,
hands and jar extended,
from the top of the cement barbeque
to the sea of patio concrete below
and scalped himself.
So when mom took the tea towel
and wiped the blood from his forehead
all his hair lifted up
like an insecure toupee.

Of course mom screamed a lot and
it took a doctor twenty stitches
to sew the stuffing
back into his head.

2.

When he was eight years old
and culpable before the Mormon god,
they decided to baptize his abnormally long body
by full immersion for the remission of his sins.

Each time they tried,   plunging him under,
a toe or finger or elbow would refuse to submerge.

For years after he was a joke with the local congregation
holding the record for the number of times
dunked before they got him right under, completely immersed,
in another place with gravity suspended.

3.

When he was about five he would wander off
whenever I was assigned to look after him.

One day in a blustery late November
I had taken him to the long beach
by Semiahmoo Bay.
I recall our large puffy parkas, mitts, boots.

Distracted by birds or agates or whips of seaweed
I forgot about him and
when I looked he was knee deep
in the wine dark sea.
And then he was waist deep neck deep
then submerged.
But every few seconds his head
would burst through the surface
blowing like a whale and then down
and relentlessly forward he'd go until
I caught up with him and
dragged him blubbering to shore.

Then one day,
years later, he suspended his tall frame
in too short a room and
immersion by gravity
a fish on a string,
received a remission of sin,
entered the gallon jar with one smooth cartoon move,
took an endless hike on the beach
at the bottom of Semiahmoo Bay.

ST MARTIN'S HALL

1.

Write an unwritten Stephen King novel. I have filled out the
application forms and taken out ads in the local newspaper.
"Notice of Change of Name"

Perhaps, leaving sleeping dogs asleep, a Stephen King novel
should be written by Stephen King, but frankly I need the
money. "Dormitory" by Stephen Noble was born. Sick way to
start; Stephen King's a terrible writer. Nevertheless, I really need
the money. See, it all fits together as tight as a knife and a wound.

2.

When I first came here full of hope, a factory of hard-ons, I was a
young student. This landscape is a desert now, but then, it was a
rain forest constantly shrouded in mist, draped in dim sheets of
persistent rain. These days, if I told a passerby that we live "in a
giant bowl with a lid on it," eyebrows would shift toward the dry
blue sky. My mental state discreetly questioned.

But once it had been the universal description of the locale and
its preoccupation with dark weather.

3.

I lived then in Room 204 St Martin's Hall. The collared Toad was
proctor and buried himself in prayer within his great room at the
hall's end~

(And what was the colour of the linoleum, who had green eyes
and how many left their pointy shoes beneath the covers at the

end of the tiny plywood dorm bed. What were their names? Do they have names now?) (Go on, Joseph Conrad, entertain us ... how many nails did you say were driven into the great hull of that wooden merchant ship? Please, describe each ... and what were their names? Could they tap dance?)

If I had a hammer. Perhaps I'd beat my precise memories to death or into a golden sheet so thin light would pass through ... elemental.

4.

Getting old is the shits. Don't let anyone paint you a golden picture. No wonder religions work on the suppression of desire and in their experiments alchemically change sexual expression into bloodshed and war. Gold to Lead.

All I have desired I still desire as I drift away into a land of mummies and memories, yet my mouth waters. A desire hard to hold for longer than an instant. And all I have loved to eat becomes deadly poison or too hard to chew with so few teeth. Those I have loved have graciously become friends.

I sit another one out. Drift back to the glories of St Martin's Hall and forget that my ass is shaped like a chair.

5.
Dear Willow,

This is about a nightmare I'm having. When I first arrived in town I was a young self-consumed romantic poet who dreamed

41

of painting masterpieces and harnessing fame. I lived for two years in St Martin's Hall, the dormitory above Studio 80 at the old University Campus. It was an interesting situation — Maple Leaf hockey players and acid-soaked hippies sharing tiny rooms along a crowded hall with one large communal shower. I managed to maintain my room as a single residence by being as rude as possible whenever administration attempted to move in a roommate. Chain smoking and horking regularly was my most effective remedy. My room was filled with candles and wood block printed curtains, the sound of Anderson Creek bubbled through the windows ... a constant stream of lovers visited and a substantial portion of my life jogged by. I lived in or near the little town for thirty years. I ran a small club of alcoholics across the street from the dormitory. I waltzed and laughed all night ... all night ... I've had a heart attack, which caused my acute awareness of mortality and its teetotalling stringencies ... and now in the paper I read that the old dorm St Martin's is slated to become economy warehousing for poor old people. So the current nightmare began ... lineups of old lovers played by Vincent Price in drag, clacking and scraping like Marley's ghost at the door of my retirement: Room 204 St Martin's.
Bits of yellow skin falling to the floor with each monkey-paw knock at my door ... all the old lovers returned with warped Moody Blues records and seedy Mexican mud pot.
I am very entertained by life. It is like a fat flower whose petals are questions ... whose calyx is a book too tiny to read even with new glasses. I am very entertained by life and its inescapable twists and tricks. Targeted, I prefer to remain uninvolved but even my neutrality is another cause in this jello-juggling riot of effects. Drop me a line when you're not so busy–T

Kathi's dead now.

FRANKENSTEIN'S SCOTTISH LAMENT

I was not loved so lashed out
with terror and my big phony mouth;
houses of old brick and dry board shook.

At the threnody shop
my head was sewn back on
with a stretched thread of blue tears.

My lungs replaced with an old set
of tartan border pipes, lions rampant,
fresh from a bloody border war.

I found an ice berg
and tore my lips off
kissing its metal lipstick.

I went to the north pole
it was no longer a candy cane
I had forgotten the name of sweetness.

I made wild plans with myself
baked strawberry pies and chocolate embraces,
no one came to my feast so I ate very well.

McCrimmon and my ascended heart visit
the sharp edge of a banshee and
drown in a lifetime that's almost over.

BESIDE ME

Although I failed to sleep as
you slept beside me,
my exhaustion a sunset
with your smooth horizon
breathing and perfect
in darkness beside me.

And the form of your body
remains an angel in the bedding
pressed wild rose petal
in the pages of some sacred text.

Your imperceptible breath,
missing, leaves empty silence
suspended, a forest ghost
of a fresh blue wind in the smoke
and yawning air around me.

Your eyes closed in my
night time memory, cupped
in a green garden sheltering
rare midnight bird song.

Your arm the gentle slope of path
rising to the crown of heaven,
you asleep, are both enigma
and epiphany, vision suspended
in my blindness, a song unsung,
as in silence so softly
you sleep, so safe you sleep beside me.

SEASON OF HISTORY

I gave up all my notes
instructions to myself
insurance of orderly activity
left them to one side
search instead for wild roses
or the ghosts of dark camps
long deserted

Construct rambling dreams
command the crows
to march the sky with a precision
that carries them nowhere

Some ask the world
to leap as fools leap
into ash and conflagration
the dangerous christian notion
of hand-made armageddon

But instead I rest here longer
wrapped by woolly winter blanket
though it is june
soon the summer will be
upon us
with the hot breath of
a circling beast
then quickly gone before
shortened evenings of autumn
dance their silhouette around the corner
subtle tai chi mourner
before the shell of tumbling winter.

JUST A GIRL

When my grandmother
raised a daughter and a neighbour's leftover son
during the decade long great depression
outside Pilot Mound Manitoba
without a cent but with a green garden and
some chickens
a sewing needle
lived in a ten-by-ten wooden shed
sheltered from dust by a windbreak
of rattling trees she'd planted
the stuttering wind called "she's just a girl"

When I was three and my drunken father
tumbled in from work
all sweat and anger
called my mom chattel
called her cooking "crap"
choked her with his stony fists ...
and my grandmother visiting
emerged from the other room,
tiny as a worn fence post
struck back
reached up and gently tapped
him on his shoulder ...
surprised
he turned and she sent an upper cut
into his eye
blackening it from socket to dropped jaw
down he sat and wept in a chair
bad boy corrected and
always humble in her presence ever after
because she was "just a girl"
When my youngest daughter at two and a half

disappeared from the barbeque party and
sent the neighbourhood searching
the road and vast forest above us
calling out "emma emma emma," and
the police were called
came to join the search and
then I found her sitting like a tiny Rodin sculpture
on a rock deep in the drapes of Emily Carr's forest,
she looked up and said,
"dad, leave me alone, i'm thinking,"
and she was "just a girl" then.

And my other daughter with
children and suicide husbands and
trailer court woes rose up and juggled it all
by herself battled
a different kind of depressed world
"just a girl" covering her beauty in a warrior face.

My eldest daughter, tiny and delicate, sparred with men for a
year in a Kelowna gym
and got herself thumped in the first professional boxing match
between women in BC, live on BCTV,
just to make sure the BC women's boxing federation
could occur   puffed up on the front page
a giant purple grape   she never fought again
securing sports territory she won for other women
then left for japan to learn the perfect arrangement of flowers
"just a girl"

When I meditate and see
the love of women surrounding me
grandmothers, mothers, daughters and lovers
the greatest value and security
the best memories and lessons
at this juncture in my lengthening life
when I hear their voices their deepest care
their patient resistance to weaker male fear
I swear they're all "just girls"

All around the whirly world everything here comes
from them and everything returns to the mother again
and she's "just a girl"
In pink or blue, or you or sitting next to you
Just a bindi in a yantra
just ruler of all tantra
all the men like muddy water caught
in the hoof print of a cow
and compared, "just a girl" … all oceans and seas
now in dance with grandmother moon

Just a girl why we breathe
who lifts us up in our death
who delivers us each life to breath
Just a girl Om krim kali ki ahmana
Just a girl Om krim kali ki ahmana
Just a girl Om krim kali ki ahmana
Just a girl kali kali kali

CLUMP

I have brought a clump
of the wildest outside earth
to my house
so the grass
and strange bestial mosses
will grow by my table

Perhaps black birds will come
as the sun rises
across my blue porridge bowl.

BODHISATTVA OF RAGS

She is a bodhisattva of rags
walking as a scarecrow appears to walk
on the horizon of lead trajectories
and barbed fence lines
the river ice breaking up into lifeboats
moving inexorably
to a warm southern ocean

She wonders how to turn away
from her old vow as if it were the lost iron anchors
of a sunken fleet forgotten in sand and seaweed
in tidal dance like
a windy green forest for Dungeness crabs
orange as taxis in ultra marine night

Her sorrow is all encompassing
like a martyr who flings her body
on the blazing crematory flame
in a disciplined display of clenched detachment
she recalls the surrender
of a passing history of weather
blowing like smoke rings or halos
across the bent fields of sad memory

She lifts up ghosts and heals them
hides notes under fieldstone
to mislead the generations
hefts the karma of isolated families
like a basket of wizened apples
in the marketplace

She weighs the sense
of their belonging nowhere
drowned grains of black tea
gathered by the frail fingers of slaves

She juggles trance and circumstance
huddles in the arms of blue northern winter
and her icicle fingers gather
dry hollow sorrow
like stale yellow corn cakes

She makes them edible
with a thin syrup of golden hope

She is the bodhisattva who collects
the tatters and rags of destiny
calls out from her wooden wagon
creaking across the flatland of her isolation:
"rags and bones and sometimes string
rags and bones and sometime spring
feathers and songs with a semblance of joy"

She dances with whisky
in a hollow leather shoe.

THE SUN AND THE SHOWER

Frank O'Hara in his manifesto says
it's either the poem or the telephone:
You, in the shower at the moment
have no access to poems or telephones
you, even though the sun was shining
through the kitchen window at ten a.m.
striking the left side of my face
warm and having that wonderful painterly effect
of making me look contemplative
to some third eye, some other person
who obviously wasn't there because
even though the sun was creating halos etc
you said, with all vehemence, that
you hate me
because i talk too much

The sun denies it
the room looks like the inside of a spring daffodil
I look like a saint in an enlightened private moment.
You must not have focused properly,
look again, when you return wet and amphibian
from the fibreglass shower, look again
the imprint may still be there
a powerful hologram, at rest in a chair

PURGATORY

I seem to be the night-watchman of purgatory
singing quiet old songs against the dead hills.
When you come near me with your echo
I don colourful shirts and try to remember a vital dance.

I have first class ferry tickets and yellow absolutions.
The halos are not here, the halos have never been here.
They are up in the attic with the abandoned gift wrap
of goodness, the wobbling promises of new wilderness.

I am never sad long but I record your hidden sadness,
acutely experience your forgotten hidden sorrow,
as I might feel an oppressive and cloying moisture in the air
hours before the advent of an engulfing downpour.

Sorrow and waiting are the two kinds of weather here
with much slow green moss for sitting,
time to patiently eye the defunct pink clock and
click out the missing "tick tock" with mouth and tongue.

I am the watchman of purgatory.
It is always deep night here and the oily coffee
tastes like old lead pencil shavings.
My friends rewrite their examinations as if they're leaving.

RESOLUTIONS

I am not going down to the lake
i will not light bonfires to the
depth of winter
i will not dance
to the songs of the ancestors
(he blessed a corner of my property
there beside the doghouse
he blessed it with smoke and his
famous smile

On another new year he shattered
his woman's skull and smoked up
the room
with bits of brain and gunpowder)
i will not burn sweetgrass
by my doghouse
i will not bless strangers before i
bless myself
i will not drink water
if it is just a ceremony
i will not love your body
in some dull ritual
i will not stand so naked
on the cold cold morning
i will speak the truth as it comes to me
occasionally
like last night's falling stars

FALSE APOLOGY

Please forgive the dry days the
mono-dimensional erotic drawings
images of women curled
sardine blow jobs in a can
while some mornings in the dark
I am a fallen man   an animal
with pomp and splendor
the musty smells of spit-buffed uniform

KATHI

asbestos tests annually
at 62 because at
19 years old
i worked
at the cassiar mine

the summer
i lost kathi
to some thug
in vernon
to another
because
of distance and slow
postal service

when I saw her
again she came
to my door
at the chit chat café
apartment
in white rock
we loved all afternoon

then she left
on a bus
and was gone

her sister
just told me
she died
and her family

thought well of me
wanted me at
the funeral

SUMMER POEM

all summer
on burnt hillside
with sienna earth   ochre shovel
rusted hoe
he bends
and with various incantations
oaths   he urges forth
the small greens
and commands black root
further to the depth
of its dark sky

all summer at the blue dawn
his coffee-eyed neighbours
watch
as in the centre
of his small eden
he feeds the crows
and speaks with their voice

how the dark birds
guard   his perfect corn

MY MOTHER DREAMED

My mother dreamed of freedom
from the farm
and fell headlong into my broken father's arms
heaving bags of wheat ...
his strong young back lithe   muscular
in the slick humidity of a Toronto summer.

My mother dreamed of freedom and
the slightly older native guy who played guitar
at Pilot Mound Manitoba dances
when she was twelve and allowed to attend.
(Seeing her
he would always put his guitar down
abandon the band and
dance her ecstatic
once around the floor)

So when I asked my mother
(submerged in the advent of dementia),
she said she had married my defeated father
instead of her true attraction
because he had a strong back,
because he was the first one
who had asked her
and it was 1949
she was already twenty
all her girl-friends had married
at seventeen and eighteen
to survivors of WWII and she
alone
had not been asked ... no proposals of roses
no elopement from the farm to a city
of civil night lights and amazing pop-up toasters,

(smouldering white bread soars
across the arborite table
to the red and yellow display
of a fried northern breakfast.)

And he asked ... the first to ask ...
A hero saving her from the prison farm
from the impending horror of old maidenhood.

And my mother dreamed,
so when he failed and failed again
retreated from her
to the drunken and skewed honour
of solitary hunter gatherer
sending the kill home by Canada Post
once a month
home a thousand miles away from his solitary job
the frozen animation
of his dark winter
below the permafrost
mining the heavy element
lead galena   fishing weight   counterfeit
poison from deep below
Keno Hill Yukon.

And my mother dreamed of freedom
when an Elder of Israel
with a drawling Utah smile
led her to total submersion
marriage to a religion of cowboy gods
who asked much by tithing and time
but did not strike her ...

Their god refrained from wine and misery
a god of opulent procreation
farmer god in an office suit
excessive god pleased
by shiny coins and the idiot
songs of hopeful children.

Oh my mother dreamed
she was the lady of the lake.
She dreamed of art galleries and
driftwood collected was carefully varnished,
drilled and turned to crafty lamp pedestals
spread out across the basement floor
to somehow redeem the failure
of a family where everyone broken
reached out to everyone broken
for the severed possibility
of a dwarfed idea of love.

We'll drill holes in this driftwood,
she said.
We'll run wires   buy fixtures.
We'll make lamps and let our little light shine.
Won't we Tim?

SUMMER CAMP

There must be a place to feed
all the scavenging things
like us dependent on
the ebb and flow
of meat   milk   ocean's fish
songs we learn to mimic.

My mother with her dementia
in a moment of great clarity mumbles
"This is pretty boring"

Then reminded she was
the great storyteller of our family
the one just starting to eat
a now cold meal
after all the others at the table
were done with eating
and her story had finally wound down ...

After mumbling disjointedly
for some minutes she says clearly
*"Even if there's only one good story
I've got to tell it"*

In our disintegration
there exist bright sparks
Shooting up to join stars
above us in a night of summer
camps, ghost stories, sing-alongs.

TAKING AIR

*The air was mild and fresh, and shone with a faint unsteadiness
that was exactly like the unsteadiness of colors inside a seashell*
— Maeve Brennan

He greeted ghosts in deserted houses,
honking the car horn
he passed the collapsed
shadows of homesteads
along the highway
on his way down.

The last full day I spent with him
we drove along Kootenay Lake
across the ferry past Pilot Bay
and on to the abandoned
Bluebell Mine   once the richest
silver mine in the old empire.
Mineshafts so deep beneath the lake
they eventually filled with water,
congested lung of stone lined
with hoards of silver still.

Years before he had worked
as the hoist-man at the silver-lead-galena mines
of the northern Yukon
and filled with that dust, bad novels, beer
endless packs of Macdonald's Export 'A'
he grew silent and turned in
on himself
victim of isolation and addiction.

He turns off and drives
the old black car
up a narrow and steep logging road
... through a golden corridor of birch and larch
up until
we can go no further and
here silently, father and son take air.

Overlooking the expanse
of Kootenay Lake
and far below them, the Bluebell Mine
filled with the ghosts of a century's
hard-working men.

Down below where
vast blue mist
leans to reveal
thin green horizon.
The heart races
stones tossed from a mountain,
world claims dimension.
No word is spoken.

First
hands in his pockets
he kicks a rock
over the edge,
down the precipice
we wait   we listen
stone heartbeat thumping
and its final distance,
muffled silence.
Father and son

Take turns   kick stones
off the edge
of the autumn mountain
until he whispers, "enough."
Turning away from the air
a return to the car
descent from the mountain
a vacuum
and then the days of ribcage calendars,
pitiful crawling from oxygen tents
for one more puff of
suffocation
silence, always silence leading to silence.

A wooden lawn chair
takes advantage of afternoon sun.
Ochre and gold burnt sienna,
umber ribcage, Gordian root.
No one returns to the empty chair.
The shadow there appears to give speeches.

DWINDLING

Age inspires the pink body to bulbous anarchy
songs sung ricochet in recesses of gourd or seashell,
lovers are always memories:

Monuments to pleasure or specific moment
lifted from mundane place — stance
or insignificance:

The baby slept as you rounded some perfectly white corner
in winter — ten years ago — the clearest
memories burst like pomegranates
reveal the sweet red core of life.

Great treasures dwindle, amount to a cheerful nothing.

OLD GLOBE

Some dreams i have are dreams
of things i do not want to happen,
of labyrinth of lost child's voice,
calling through
a thick maze of laurel hedge

Vacations spent consulting lawyers
in humid hotel rooms
above the breeze
of some distant beach

Places i didn't visit
cafes where i wouldn't eat

Where no one eats

I dream this through
a green and greasy window
enter, place my order
eat and eat and eat
of synchronous tragedy,
tapestry of elizabethan horror
pit bulls in the throat
arrows in the kingly eye
rain on the stage at the
old globe   the old globe

NIAGARA

I am water walked upon
by some goddess or frail saint

A still lake quivering
after the advent of
the skipping stone

If I could be a waterfall
I would name myself Niagara
and appoint defiant
tightrope walkers to the dance
of tiny spiders above me

If I could be a waterfall
I would sing your name religiously
look away from your eyes
the lead singer in an autistic choir

STARLINGS

These dark boots pulverize
wet brown leaves underfoot
in the rain at nightfall and dabbling
with the mystery of my future:

How like the rain my fear of the flood
constant and on the grey night edge
a fermented chorus of aggressive starlings
drag my heart like food toward
the absolute mouth of another morning.

CODES

We speak to each other in a code,
our moment a recipe of cakes and crows
We sing our distant song
without black telephones and
there is no other place to go
as in the distance she needs to hew
a soft wall of fixed vision,
snow monument to
the several freedoms of slavery

She is like a cat in the trees.
She makes enigmatic faces and pretends
to be blind, deaf, empty ...
or stands like a shadow silently,
or is simple geography
like a low carpet of wild ginger

So she cannot be seen. I never see her.
She is a cat static as a slow grown forest,
crouched like a soft green plant
below the distraction
of vaulted canopy and galloping weather

And I cook in the kitchen of my
departed grandmother ... or any kitchen ...
conversant with a Siamese cat
who eats shrimp sitting down
each red crustacean gripped
in one paw gracefully
nibbled on like a tiny party sandwich ...

And this cat has the mannerism
of a person and the woman
who acts like a cat in the forest
and appears to be a tree
or wild carpet of lush ginger treasured
is held in a hollow of cakes and crows;
The secret patience of bread rising.
A freedom of isolation; Enough to suffer.

WOUNDING THE ROBIN

There are potentially perfect days
when off on a search for her
voice or gesture
as seen in natural cycle
nothing displaced it, made it less
than it seemed until
the instant and a low flying robin
sucked beneath my speeding car
observed, in rear-view mirror:
autumnal feathers flutter to asphalt
the robin stumbles through its favourite air
to dark tree shadow and slow stuttering death

And then
the magic dissipated, points out imperfect clouds
the inkblot of them on watercolour sky
sun a throbbing robin's breast
trees turned up birds claw and
again he has not found a portion of godhood
in this morass of imminent death
dust rinsed daily
from aching crooked hands and limbs

Again the road shows its curves
where the map says it's straight

CANTO

wait's newsstand july

The hot still air fills
the narrow interior of wait's newsstand

It is near midnight
forest fires rampant in the region
and the lake is   still   is
so stiff and warm
that fragile pin-legged insects
traverse its width
skate   from southern to northern shore
deep in densest july
the hot air fills
the narrow interior of one small
matchbox, newsstand, coffee counter ...

The waitress with the temper skitters
from sink to pot, the coffee thick as night
and equally as hot.

EMPTY CUP

Someone removed
the saran wrap
from a macaroni casserole,
allowed it to pick up
fridge flavours,
become dry and hard
on the top, inedible,
breeding mystery
malignancies,
moon reminiscent of food,
blue cheese
withered and waning before us.

And that is how it is
suddenly, my atmosphere
stripped away within your silence,
and instead, where
once you were the weather,
the air is sterile
still and burns
like too much salt and an empty cup.

ANGEL OF BLIGHT

Maybe you should just do it tonight
so you can sit in a box all day tomorrow.

While the world ended
in fluorescence and phoney white
some chose to clutch thin candles
against interminable night

Some chose the bleak announcement
of rattling party horns
pronouncing their tiny crumbs of joy,
brief sunshine in a storm

Some fucked like no tomorrow
and some didn't fuck at all
while they waited for the orders
and cowered within their walls

And while the world ended
one sat in a room, alone,
dreaming of bridal veils
the soft song of a groom

A groom and his celebration
a bride in her flight of veils
circled the sky as black birds
tossed like ships with sails

And while the world ended
all danced and danced again,
some sang like dirty angels
in a choir of the pained

Their voices cardboard and ribbon
sputtered to false dawn
the Angel of Blight directed there
with the hook on his baton

While the world ended
some still bowed to ancient dreams
begged their gods for magic
from forgotten former scenes

And when the world ended
one spoke on a dead telephone
called out for bridal veils
in the sweet voice of a groom

Sad groom and his calculations
cold bride in her flight of veils
circled the sky as black birds
tossed like ships with sails

And outside in the corridor,
way down a deadened hall,
someone took their hard-on
and beat a heart to hell

EXTINCTIONS

My brother could not eat spaghetti
without wearing it.

Metaphorically this repeated itself
through each treadmill day of his life.

Until one day he hung himself
like a big noodle
dropped onto a crooked branch
by a raucous frolic of crows.

MARIANNE APARTMENT MALBOWGE

In this small apartment
with my chain-smoking young daughter
a view of the inner parking lot obscures
the mountain   the great cold lake called cocytus
with its frozen orange bridge

I know all this is just beyond
that window with the neighbour's
imprisoned cat

The courtyard   flat hot asphalt
black as the moustache of the man
pacing back and forth
filled with prying questions
calling out nosey parker observations
to other tenants who scurry from door to blue door
inside the square hard labyrinth

A hundred lactating women in long soiled nightgowns
are beaten each morning
by beery reeling husbands

I hear their screams
their doors slam like cannons
amplified through my diaphanous walls

I watch as these husbands
with shovels and wrenches and greasy muscles
stride across the big hard lot
to some distant work, and return
from that mindless netherworld clutching
new beer   tobacco   and dirt

wallets filled
with squares of stolen toilet paper

Midday in the hot sun the same
seven children play   make an animated game
of shrieking   "fuck you"
and now the blue doors are silent
plain linen curtains do not move

The neighbour's air conditioner in the apartment above
drips water on my windowsill all day long   incessant
I have seen this kind of rain before

BIRCH BARK TOYOTA

I drive the seasonal Toyota
down night's long highway
Toyota white as
the ghost
of a birch tree

We travel home
It is two a.m.
think of the
perfectly enclosed room
pleased   in the picture
drive on and
see John on Patmos
post-anachronistic session
with an angelic host
he is exhausted
not from sightseeing
but from the
greasy mechanics of wrenching
ancient concepts
from the machine of eternity

I drive the quick white Toyota
The road a slow motion carnival
Sandman in the back seat yawns
beckons to have me yawn or sneeze

But my body
moves perfectly
foot commands accelerator
hand with magician flicks

the wheel twirls
guides the now mythic vehicle
forward to its destination

Suspicious eyes of animals
deep in the shadow forest
pierce hedges of
scotch broom   ditch weed
sounds of creeping
night shut outside
this sacred speeding microcosm
my metal animal   brother of locust and
gaseous wormwood
perfect machine
of whirring landscape

Thank you for my microcosm
the perfect machine
highway visions
thank you for rewarding me
with both sides of the centre line
each night past midnight

BEYOND THE SUICIDE

for Me-No-Whe-Ka-Mi-Ki-Nung
of the Ojibway Nation

Here we have the grainy but static
manifestation of the perfect woodsman
as he clutches his cornucopia of hissing hubric fruit

Here the beloved suicide smiling
from ear to missing ear — so suddenly
headless — yet deep in dream beyond the scrambled brain
ceiling

Listening for the dull drum of some disturbed vision of grouse
muscles sore — head so very light and no true mirror
no true mirror or hope of examination

Only the hollow brainless thought
(brains disassembled — embedded in drywall or yellow
sponge — finally deep in some septic of piss and pinesol)

His false remembrance of murdering everything
of breaking the children's colourful toys
of living after we all had died

And he has become the bright tooth knocked out unwillingly
the good song on paper burnt up in drunken fire
for him we view the night stars and blow smoke

To the house of summer and the stark plain of winter
to the bed of the sun and to its morning rising — to him
bone powder beyond the quadrants of this green bowl that holds us

THE MESS

I feel empty. The world was
a mess when I was born
men shooting men
men shooting women and as I grew I
was given a toy gun and all my young friends
received toy guns and then the children
shot the children and I also got my mom
right in the eye I poked her and
shouted "gotcha!!"

And she had a black eye for a long time
and removed my toy gun
and the children said "That's OK,
you can still play, we need an Indian."

RAVENS

A cluster of darkling winter ravens
move like a net across the red-grey snow sky
circle — careen — look for sleeping heads to catch
to net — to drag to sudden flight
above the blank white of a hundred
square rooftops huffing their winter fuel out
in brown breath
inside dreamers eat dinner — curl in red blanket
pass the plate — the sweet and meat
and sleep and sleep while ravens
passing like a net — do not hesitate
never waver in their undulation
their synoptic formation

BETHLEHEM

There was one small town with romance at every bend
we all passed through
we saw each other there

My grandfather murdered himself
my father murdered himself
i am from a long line of murderers
should i not carry on the tradition?

There was one small town with beautiful flesh in all the windows
we all watched as the perspiring bodies danced
their circus dance
we felt each other's warm breath on the night air

My grandfather was a prisoner to ships that sailed in bottles
my father was a prisoner of meaningless smoke signals
i am just a prisoner — no secret delineations

And in the night i see you walking
looking for a map
looking for the mail that will announce it
looking for godiva on some multiseated horse
looking for a saviour to pin it on
looking for some bethlehem and those angels
that walking around with mules and virgins
look like common men

PANDORA'S GINGERBREAD

Its big stone jar of evil habits
Has smashed in a million pieces. — *Kabir*

Piñata are usually pleasing
paper images of happy donkeys
jubilant wagging dogs
stuffed with candy
they deliver
in a beneficent shower
when the object of beauty
that contains them
is sufficiently beaten
by blind people with sticks,
torn and broken wide open,
ruptured membrane of tiny blessing,
sugary internal organs scattered,
a casting of seed.

The idea of reward emanating
from the destruction of festive beauty
might be relieved if
piñatas adopted designs
like "Hitler's yelling head."
But then, why would candy
blow out of his mouth
if not to lure
more gingerbread children
to the vaulting ovens of memory?

SAILOR'S KNOTS

Everyone's friend, you know him,
always hanging around
in the background
quiet guy, a bit stiff,
a bit grim, came to me
and said "Hey Tim let's tour,
bit of a walk,"
a Dickensian cane,
reluctant re-workings
of an obscured brain,
"give me some proofs of how
your killing began,
what you killed, some why and when,
your dealings with weapons
from birth to death,
your arsenal, your aim
and what they imply"

Always my own first victim
I built the glass house in Creston
with empty amber embalmer's bottles and
nervously smoked four hundred
fifty-one thousand two hundred and fifty cigarettes

In the gaudy greens, flashing reds
of midnight café neon light
and the blue smoke
of forty-eight thousand
one hundred and twenty joints,
which failed to kill
even the most inconsequential
memory, and the
seven hundred acid trips like bullets

aimed at everyone's versions of god
bounced off at the feet of John Cage
tinkling chains of sterling coins belly dancers wear

As a child I imprisoned bright butterflies
in glass jars because I loved them
they suffocated
At four I planted gardens and
sacrificed the aghast faces of
a crowd of pansies to the mouth of ever
impending Canadian winter

Poked holes in a jar lid
captured more rare butterflies
because I loved them
they died
I found them there   sleeping beauties
in a bed of shredded grass
and yellow leaves

Later a seabird was killed with stones
swam in circles with broken neck
drown
submerged to the immeasurable depth
of my pea-sized heart
became my albatross
and then   bolstered with the intent
of some primal genetic memory
in a tricky hunter moment
I stole crumbs of
Mormon sacramental bread
put them beneath a tall pine tree

and waited at distance
for the chirpy squirrel to descend
then threw my Jim Bowie brand
hunter's knife
bonked it on the head
with the butt end and
it screamed and ran up the tree
and flopped around until it hung
by one paw
from a branch
at a great elevation
dead

I will not go on to individually list
the many I have killed to eat
chickens, turkeys, pigs and fish
screaming crabs in a boiling dish

I murdered the heart
of my several marriages ...
lovers turned away, forgotten
pages of a passing novel ...
homes burned behind me
celebrations of
a conqueror's disastrous passage

Loved too much so greedily
arranged the death of marriage
with the phoney innocence
of the weapon of poetry

I created a resting place
for death and old memory
simply going for an evening walk
with my newspaper and my sad intent.
And now for you, old familiar, a bit of a hike,
a climb and decline with Dickensian cane,
two crooked old crows dressed
in the dark suit of night

You tell me our next tour of collapse
must soon proceed   the yellow fields,
the smoke and ash of harvest fires,
the clay and the hill and the recollection there
of all the dancers   reach out
with a ribbon at the finish line,
fluttering like a highway on a paper map,
one long string tied in sailor's knots
suspend the bodies both innocent and albatross

CAW

There is darkness coming
now at evening
a cusp of moon in the dusk
all gold silver and flaking rust
falls like bricks
of old town upon
simple pedestrian street

Uplookers frozen at the sight
of these particles of nothing
this sheet of night
snoring its stitches
black holes for no reason
all gold and silver and rust
crunch of the fallen underfoot
pallid husk abandoned

By surgery of dancing crows
dark wings   rose hips
memory of a rose

RECORDS

for Emma Shay

It was important to the beach
that I be there each morning
bent and walking slowly
in search of a remnant of stone history

It was important that the baby learn.
to walk, to hear
in the circled realm of screeling birds
birds she would grow to love
to record methodically
in her little lined book
as we record the junctures
of indecisive lives
anomalies that teach
a hunter's still wariness

The beach yields visions and secrets
my child's eyes pinned
like butterflies to the collection
of rolling sky

BUGGY ACCIDENT

plunging down the gravel strip
galloped by he saw the moon
rise
and fence-posted that buggy full-speed
without control
exploded
a roman candle
at some rodeo

this john wayne
like jesse fell

and there was no audience
but for the moment
his leather hat
the round moon
they were no different

two light pigskin circles
twirled by
and all the spokes
like frenzied chopsticks
in a chinese nightmare
flew past
his gaped mouth
and no audience
for his travelling

the moment prior to impact
to smashed teeth
on that hardest gravel
the moment before he thought
in the corner of his spinning

eye — he saw — a tv crew
ready to announce
his small cataclysm
his falling cowboy sky
and in wet scarlet
prone on hard road
he static   saw
the locomotion of his horse's ass
harness ribboned and waving
a thousand distant goodbyes

BLACK POEM

I dreamed of my father
young and thin
how black his car was in '55
how black his hair
raven and oilslick
vaseline and weekend brylcreem
dream of my father
how i could not
imagine his copulation
how i could not imagine copulation
then   small
contained by suspender and crew-cut
filled with the memoryless
locomotion of a young child learning ...

Fathers tall and black smoke long
across the grey industrial end:
the meat factories and their
cacophonic carcass scent
spread like death or old mustard
on our somnolent suburb
while father in his black socks
(most easily seen by me)
mounted his black car
on its asphalt
and searched out my mother
from deep in the twinkling jungle
of a woodward's store.

Yes i dreamed of my father
young and thin
a dapper man without a grin
(my tiny anger growing even then)

as with keyhole saw he cut
a tiny plywood dog
planted it sullenly on the lawn
memorial to my live dog dead
goldie deep in the flowerbed
run over by transit in '54
twenty feet from darkwood door.

CRAB SHELL

The ocean calls me back
ghosts of my hometown now true ghosts
or survivors
the nerds and beauties of my struggle
through grade-school

The stony beach
soft snore of nearby volcanoes
women who remember fish and chips
and tiny transistor radios
the deep fear of being tossed off the pier
by a local Elvis Presley

Ghosts of my hometown call to explore
make peace with my early terror
with the death of love
while steep hills invite kamikaze drivers
down down to the long stretch
of parking and freight trains
trumpeting foghorns   Semiahmoo bay
ghost ship and flowerbeds
of orange crab shell discarded

FIRST ANNIVERSARY OF MY MOTHER'S DEATH

On the bus to White Rock
I thought about my years there
Remembered my mother
moving in and out of my life
as several forms of weather

Disappointed at the White Rock Museum
I released some of my unexpressed grief
claimed the world was not right and
this was in fact the worst museum
no museum at all
and only cut my rampage short
when I noted tears welling up
in the young curator's eyes

I had an oyster burger
at moby dick's
two cold beer
because the day seemed preternaturally hot

On the rocky beach
dead baby crab shells normally bleached
washed by sea and rain
had baked and were a bright enamel red
I took a photo of them lined up like cars

Walking up the steep hills
to the bus stop
I paused in my old alley   stood
in the thick shade of a green laurel hedge
and watched a sparrow sitting on a branch
of the old Bing cherry tree
(pastoral habitation of ancient summers)

... watched the still sparrow when
without warning it toppled over
hit the hot asphalt with a small thump
sputtered and trembled for a second
then died talons up   wide eyed
On the crowded slow bus home
another passenger squeezes in next to me
and the heat from his body
generates some hatred

PREVIOUSLY PUBLISHED

BOOK

This Cabin as the S.S. Titanic, poetry, Solstice Books

CHAPBOOKS

The Great Ottawa Sojourn, Elephant Mountain Press
!Fire Fireman Fire!, Elephant Mountain Press
Lament, Poetry Broadsheet, 52 pickup series, Dreadnaught Press
Fathers, Elephant Mountain Press
The Deadman's Float, Freeform Press
Bonsai, Broadsheet, Chameleon Fire Editions
Resolutions, Chameleon Fire Editions
Bodhisattva of Rags, Elephant Mountain Press
Starlings, Broadsheet, Elephant Mountain Press

ANTHOLOGIES

A Government Job at Last, Macleod Books
Alive at the Center, Ooligan Press

SOME OF THE POEMS IN THIS COLLECTION HAVE PREVIOUSLY APPEARED IN:

Grain, ("Summer Poem"); *Canadian Dimension*, ("Summer Poem"); *Zest*, ("Crow in his Dark Uniform"); *Writing Magazine*, ("Bethlehem"); *Scrivener*, ("Black Poem", "Monsters"); *Quarry*, ("Wounding the Robin"); *CV2*, ("The Sun and the Shower"); *Newest Review*, ("Canto: Wait's News, July"); *This Magazine*, ("Resolutions"); *Rift*, ("Marianne Apartment Malbowge", "Season of History"); *Horsefly*, ("Angel of Blight", "Beside Me", "Pandora's Gingerbread"); *Qwerty*, ("Codes", "Purgatory"); *Post-Feminist-Post*, ("Just a Girl").

ACKNOWLEDGMENTS

A tip of the hat to my muses, my mentors, my loves, the ancestors, my family, the quantum and the crow.

With thanks to the writers of Vancouver for their welcoming care and inclusion.

Special thanks to the owners of Hogan's Alley Café.

Thank you, Alisha Weng, for the author's photograph.

Appreciation, love, and thanks, to George Payerle for his precise and passionate editorial work, and to Dennis E. Bolen, friend and compatriot.

Some of these poems were written with the assistance of the Canada Council.

TIMOTHY SHAY has contributed to numerous chapbooks and magazines, including *CV2*, *Grain*, *The Fiddlehead*, *This Magazine* and *Rolling Stone*. His work has aired on CBC Radio and been anthologized, most recently in *Alive at the Center: Contemporary Poets of the Pacific Northwest* (Ooligan Press, 2011). His first book, *This Cabin as the S.S. Titanic* was published in 1984.

This book is set in Arno Pro, designed by Robert Slimbach.
The text was typeset by Amy Thuy Do and Vici Johnstone.
Caitlin Press, Spring 2016.
❧